Looking at . . . Procompsognathus
A Dinosaur from the TRIASSIC Period

THE NEW DINOSAUR COLLECTION

For a free color catalog describing Gareth Stevens' list of high-quality books and multimedia programs, call 1-800-542-2595 (USA) or 1-800-461-9120 (Canada). Gareth Stevens Publishing's Fax: (414) 225-0377. See our catalog, too, on the World Wide Web: http://gsinc.com

Library of Congress Cataloging-in-Publication Data

Freedman, Frances.
    Looking at— Procompsognathus / by Frances Freedman; illustrated
by Tony Gibbons. — North American ed.
        p. cm. — (The new dinosaur collection)
    Includes index.
    Summary: Provides information about how the procompsognathus,
a small carnivore that lived during the Triassic Period, may have looked
and behaved.
    ISBN 0-8368-1734-6 (lib. bdg.)
    1. Procompsognathus—Juvenile literature. [1. Procompsognathus.
2. Dinosaurs.] I. Gibbons, Tony, ill. II. Title. III. Series.
QE862.S3F74   1997
567.9′7—dc20   96-41853

This North American edition first published in 1997 by
Gareth Stevens Publishing
1555 North RiverCenter Drive, Suite 201
Milwaukee, Wisconsin 53212 USA

This U.S. edition © 1997 by Gareth Stevens, Inc. Created with original © 1996 by Quartz Editorial Services, 112 Station Road, Edgware HA8 7AQ U.K.

Consultant: Dr. David Norman, director of the Sedgwick Museum of Geology, University of Cambridge, England.

Additional artwork by Clare Heronneau.

Printed in the United States of America

1 2 3 4 5 6 7 8 9 01 00 99 98 97

Looking at . . .
Procompsognathus
A Dinosaur from the TRIASSIC Period

by Frances Freedman

Illustrated by Tony Gibbons

THE NEW
DINOSAUR
COLLECTION

Gareth Stevens Publishing
MILWAUKEE

Contents

Introducing
Procompsognathus

Most people think that all dinosaurs were huge. But that is not the case. In fact, one of the first dinosaurs to evolve, **Procompsognathus** (<u>PROH</u>-KOMP-SOG-<u>NAY</u>-THOOS), was one of the smallest that paleontologists have discovered so far — much smaller than *you* are! And it is also one of the "stars" of *The Lost World*, author Michael Crichton's sequel to *Jurassic Park*.

And could **Procompsognathus**, such as the two pictured *above*, protect themselves from larger predatory creatures?

We invite you to read on and get to know these amazing little creatures. Scientists have not found many of their fossilized remains, but they still know quite a bit about them.

So what did **Procompsognathus** look like? Where was it found? Was it an herbivore or a carnivore?

5

Pint-sized

Only about 4 feet (1.2 meters) long, **Procompsognathus** was one of the smallest dinosaurs ever discovered. It was only about half your height, so you could have sat under its tail, just like the boy in this illustration. But, of course, no humans existed at the time of the dinosaurs. And, although it was just pint-sized by dinosaur standards, **Procompsognathus** was a greedy, predatory carnivore.

Procompsognathus was light on its feet, and it could probably get around very quickly. This means it was probably a successful hunter. It might also have scavenged on the remains of dead animals that had been killed by larger beasts.

Although **Procompsognathus** was not huge, many smaller creatures would have been wary of it.

Procompsognathus's prey would have had to keep alert and listen for its approach.

predator

We do not know for sure what sort of sound **Procompsognathus** made. Chances are, since it was a small dinosaur, that it produced a high-pitched noise instead of a roar or bellow.

Just imagine how noisy the Triassic world must have been with all the **Procompsognathus** squeaking at the same time!

Little and light

When paleontologists find scattered remains instead of a complete skeleton, their task is like trying to solve a jigsaw puzzle. The problem, though, is that they have no illustration on a box to guide them as they try to put the bones together. Also, many pieces are probably missing. Therefore, they have to use both their knowledge and their imagination to get an idea of what the dinosaur may have looked like all those millions of years ago.

Scientists have found very few remains of **Procompsognathus**. Our artist's reconstruction of its skeleton has been based upon both the fossilized bones that have been discovered and also the remains of similar dinosaurs.

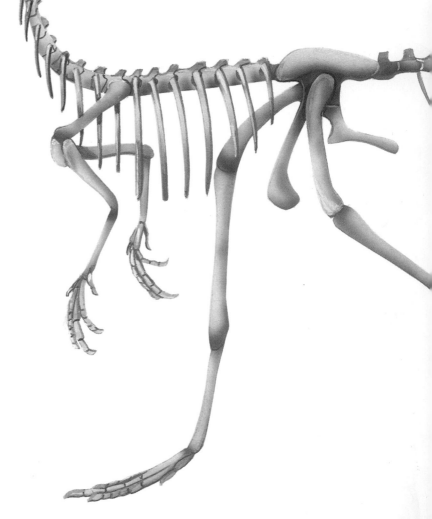

You were probably surprised to see how small **Procompsognathus** was on the previous page. In fact, if it had survived to the present day, it might have made a good pet — except that it had so many sharp teeth.

Its jaws were probably long for a creature of such a small size, and they would have been lined with lots of tiny teeth — maybe twice as many as *you* have in *your* mouth.

We know **Procompsognathus**'s skeleton must have been light-weight, because its bones were slim instead of sturdy. It probably weighed only about as much as a football.

Procompsognathus's teeth would have been very sharp. In fact, they were ideal for a daily menu of raw flesh.

We also know that **Procompsognathus** must have been bipedal. This means that it walked around on two legs instead of four. We can tell this because of the great difference between the size of its front and hind limbs.

Experts believe **Procompsognathus** had five fingers on each hand, and that two of these were shorter than the others and were used as thumbs. These may have helped **Procompsognathus** grasp and hold the prehistoric insects and other small creatures it caught for food.

In 1909, paleontologists digging in a stone quarry near a town now called Heilbron in Germany came across some fascinating remains.

They had not unearthed a complete skeleton, but the broken parts of a skull, right leg, hip, and other fossilized bones they did find were enough to show that this was an entirely new dinosaur.

In addition, it dated from Triassic times, when dinosaurs first evolved.

Later named **Procompsognathus**, it is one of several different-looking species of dinosaurs that have been discovered in this part of Europe. You can see it *below* with a **Plateosaurus** (<u>PLAT</u>-EE-OH-<u>SAW</u>-RUS) — a long-necked plant-eater that was more than six times the size of a **Procompsognathus**.

discoveries

Other interesting fossil finds that have been unearthed in Germany include five specimens of **Archaeopteryx** (<u>AR</u>-KEE-<u>OP</u>-TER-RICKS). These also date from Triassic times, so they are about 160 million years old. The remains show that this creature, which some experts say is the earliest-known bird, was about 3 feet (1 meter) long with sharp teeth and three clawed fingers on each wing, as shown in the illustration *above*. **Archaeopteryx** probably had feathers, but it could not fly well. Instead, it merely flapped its wings weakly to move around from tree to tree, constantly looking for nuts and seeds to eat.

Millions of years later, in Cretaceous times, what is now Germany was also home to the herbivore **Iguanodon** (IG-<u>WA</u>-NO-DON), most famous for its spiked thumb weapons, and also the gigantic, thick-necked carnivore **Megalosaurus** (<u>MEG</u>-A-LOW-<u>SAW</u>-RUS). They are pictured here together. The land that is now Germany has certainly played host to a wide variety of prehistoric creatures.

Death by

High above, a young **Procompsognathus** was climbing over tall rocks when it caught sight of the lake below. How inviting and refreshing the water seemed!

The sun had not long risen, but it was already a warm Triassic day. The morning light was dancing over the lake where a turtle-like **Proganochelys** (<u>PROH</u>-GAN-<u>OCK</u>-EL-EES) was fishing for breakfast.

And how tiny **Proganochelys** looked, even though it was the same size as **Procompsognathus.**

drowning

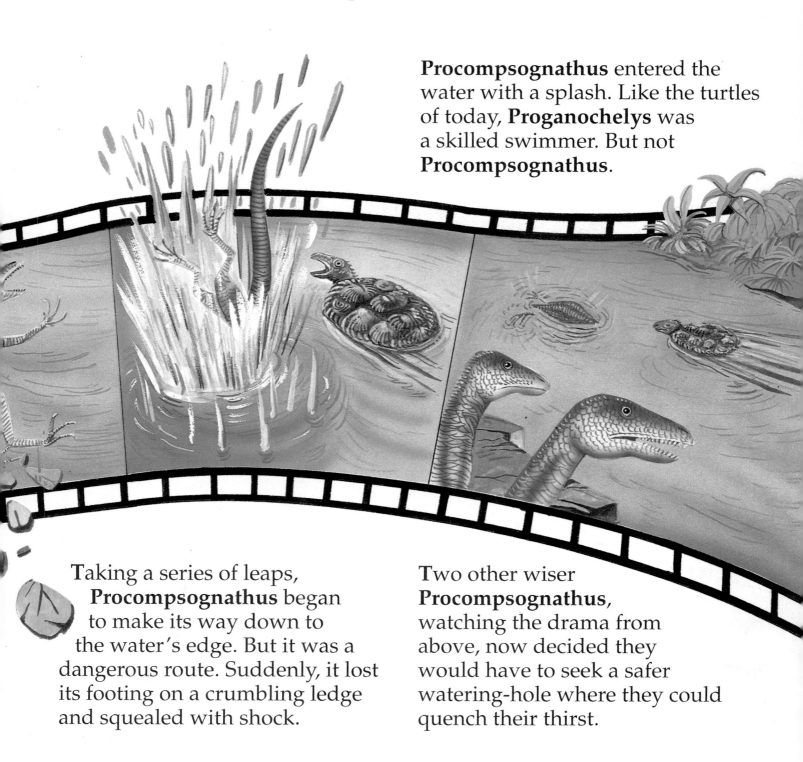

Procompsognathus entered the water with a splash. Like the turtles of today, **Proganochelys** was a skilled swimmer. But not **Procompsognathus**.

Taking a series of leaps, **Procompsognathus** began to make its way down to the water's edge. But it was a dangerous route. Suddenly, it lost its footing on a crumbling ledge and squealed with shock.

Two other wiser **Procompsognathus**, watching the drama from above, now decided they would have to seek a safer watering-hole where they could quench their thirst.

All about size

The skeletons of small, lightweight dinosaurs broke up fairly easily and quickly after they died. The bones of big dinosaurs were much tougher. This is probably why so few fossil fragments of small dinosaurs have been found in comparison with the number of skeletons of larger dinosaurs that have been unearthed.

But being small can have some advantages. Large, carnivorous dinosaurs would certainly have posed a threat and been able to defend themselves. But there were not so many of them, experts believe. Like the larger creatures of today, they did not produce many young. Small dinosaurs, on the other hand, probably had lots of babies at frequent intervals.

Smaller dinosaurs — like the three **Procompsognathus** and the baby in this scene — would also have found it no problem to run away quickly from danger.

It would also have been easier for them to climb slopes or camouflage themselves among foliage, maybe even crouching to hide.

Yet smaller creatures usually have a shorter lifespan than larger ones. A mouse, for instance, generally lives for between one and two years, while an elephant can live for thirty or forty years. So **Procompsognathus** may not have lived as long as a larger Triassic dinosaur, such as **Plateosaurus**.

Through the eyes of Procompsognathus

Pretend, for a moment, that you are a **Procompsognathus**. What would the Triassic landscape have looked like to you, all those millions of years ago?

The climate was very warm then; and in places where there were no deserts, giant conifers seemed to tower in the sky. Elsewhere, cycads and ginkgoes formed a lower canopy over an undergrowth of horsetails and ferns. This meant that a dinosaur of your size could easily find shelter both from predators and from the searing heat of a Triassic afternoon.

And what about other life-forms that walked or swam in Earth's vast forests and lakes? Tiny mammals and turtles, such as those in this illustration, would have been no threat to you at all.

But a flesh-eating theropod such as the **Halticosaurus** (HAL-TICK-OH-SAW-RUS) in the picture — although not enormous by dinosaur standards — was like a bigger version of you and so would have seemed large.

As a tiny **Procompsognathus**, you would certainly have had to keep your eyes open for these huge meat-eaters, which would have thought of you as a very tasty meal!

High above you, meanwhile, were small reptiles with wings of skin, able to glide from tree to tree. And you would have gazed in wonder at the very first pterosaurs. These were winged creatures that could soar through the skies with ease. Watch out! There's one swooping down right now in your direction, and it's even bigger than you are!

Now meet "pretty jaw"

Although they have very similar names, were both small carnivores, and at first glance looked alike, the dinosaurs **Procompsognathus** and **Compsognathus** (<u>COMP</u>-SOG-<u>NAY</u>-THOOS) actually differed in several ways.

Procompsognathus, a Triassic dinosaur, was given its name, meaning "before **Compsognathus**," by a famous paleontologist, Eberhard Fraas. **Compsognathus** was also discovered in Germany, but in Jurassic rock layers that developed much later in time. It was given a name meaning "pretty jaw." **Procompsognathus**'s name, then, means *before* pretty jaw." It is unlikely, though, that they seemed very "pretty" to the creatures that fell victim to the sharp teeth that lay within the long snouts of these mini-predators.

Compsognathus was about 2.5 feet (75 cm) long — even smaller than **Procompsognathus**. Experts have described it as being chicken-like in size. Scientists even once confused its remains with those of the first bird, **Archaeopteryx.**

Compsognathus had only two complete fingers and an extra tiny one. So it probably could not grasp its prey as well as **Procompsognathus** could. Therefore, it may have had to swallow some of its meals in one great gulp.

Some more

Experts recognized that tiny **Procompsognathus** (1) was a new discovery, mainly because of two factors — the Triassic rock layers in which it was found and the size of its remains. But several other dinosaurs looked very much like it.

All were slender meat-eaters with long jaws and sharp teeth, but they varied in size. No one knows how they may have differed in color, so our illustrator has had to guess the shade of each dinosaur's skin. **Halticosaurus** (2), with a name meaning "nimble lizard," was unearthed in Germany, as was **Procompsognathus**. It also lived during Late Triassic times.

look-alikes

Halticosaurus was also a carnivore and very large — over five times as long, in fact, as **Procompsognathus** and measuring about 18 feet (5.5 m) in length. **Coelophysis** (<u>SEEL</u>-OH-<u>FEYE</u>-SIS) (**3**), as you can see, was another Triassic look-alike, about 10 feet (3 m) long, and about the height of today's average man. **Coelophysis** was found in what is now Arizona and New Mexico.

One special feature about **Coelophysis** is that it may have been a cannibal. Scientists believe this is the case because of tiny bones from the same species that they have found in the stomach cavity of its skeletal remains. **Segisaurus** (<u>SEG</u>-EE-<u>SAW</u>-RUS) (**4**) was also a carnivore but only about the size of a goose. Its name means "canyon lizard." It was also found in Arizona, but dates from Early Jurassic times. It was therefore a later dinosaur than the other three look-alikes in the dinosaur parade shown here.

3

4

Procompsognathus

Scientists hope to find additional **Procompsognathus** remains in the future. If they do discover more complete skeletons, this would, of course, give us extra information about this dinosaur.

Let's look again at what we know about **Procompsognathus** at this point in time. Since they were so small, they probably traveled in packs. A group of them would have stood more chance of survival against an enemy. And, naturally, in packs they would have been able to hunt for food more successfully, surrounding a victim and going for the kill from all directions.

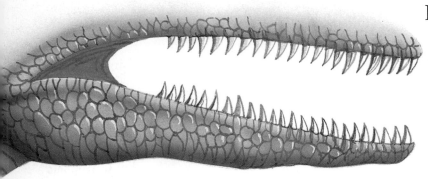

Long, tooth-lined jaws
For its size, as you can see, *left*, **Procompsognathus** had long jaws. And just look at all those teeth! Experts describe it as a meat-eater; but because of its small size, **Procompsognathus** probably did not attack larger creatures unless in a pack. When eating alone, it probably preferred to catch small lizards or insects for its snacks and meals.

data

Fleet of foot

In comparison with its small body size, **Procompsognathus** had fairly long leg and foot bones, so it was probably a fast runner and very athletic in general. We also know that it was bipedal. This means that it moved around on two legs instead of using all four limbs.

Slim tail

Procompsognathus's slim, tapering tail was probably about the same length as its body. As **Procompsognathus** ran along, it would probably have held its tail up above ground level.

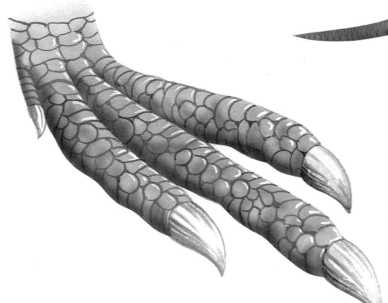

Grasping hands

From its bones, scientists can tell that **Procompsognathus** had fingers well-suited for grasping at the end of its forelimbs. Two of the five fingers on each hand were smaller than the others and may have been used like our thumbs.

Most scientists assume that **Procompsognathus** moved on two limbs mainly because its arms were so much shorter than its legs. You can see one of its feet *above*.

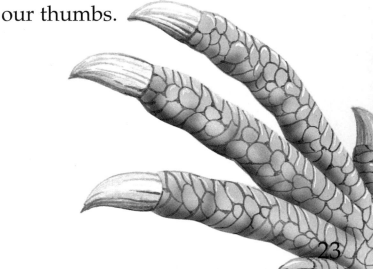

23

GLOSSARY

cannibals — animals that eat others of their own kind. The dinosaur **Coelophysis** may have been a cannibal.

carnivores — meat-eating animals.

cycads — tropical shrubs or trees that look like thick-stemmed palms.

evolve — to change or develop gradually from one form to another.

fossils — traces or remains of plants and animals found in rock.

ginkgoes — trees with showy, fan-shaped leaves and yellow fruit.

herbivores — plant-eating animals.

pack — a group of similar or related animals that travel or hunt together.

paleontologists — scientists who study the remains of plants and animals that lived millions of years ago.

predators — animals that kill other animals for food.

prey — animals that are killed for food by other animals.

scavengers — animals that eat the leftovers or carcasses of other animals.

INDEX